Crime and Racial Harassment in Asian-run Small Shops: The Scope for Prevention

Paul Ekblom and Frances Simon
with the assistance of Sneh Birdi

CRIME PREVENTION UNIT: PAPER 15
LONDON: HOME OFFICE

Editor: Kevin Heal
Home Office Crime Prevention Unit
50 Queen Anne's Gate
London SW1H 9AT

881721

Crime Prevention Unit Papers

The Home Office Crime Prevention Unit was formed in 1983 to promote preventive action against crime. It has a particular responsibility to disseminate information on crime prevention topics. The object of the present series of occasional papers is to present analysis and research material in a way which should help and inform practitioners whose work can help reduce crime.

ISBN 0 86252 348 6

Foreword

The Asian run corner shop or convenience store is now a feature of most urban areas whether they are multiracial in character or have few other members of the ethnic minorities. Too little is known about the experiences of this part of the retail sector: in particular, there is a lack of systematic information about their experience of crime and racially-offensive behaviour. This gap in our knowledge is significant because shops are at the social and economic heart of most communities, and understanding and if possible reducing the exposure of this group of shops to crime and racially offensive incidents must help them to develop as a vital element in the enterprise movement and in strategies aimed at improving neighbourhood life in inner cities and elsewhere.

This report describes the findings of a survey of Asian shopkeepers running small retail stores conducted in four widely differing areas of London, and whose aims include: obtaining a picture of the problem of crime and racially offensive behaviour; describing the range of preventive measures shopkeepers currently employ and their sources of advice; determining whether ethnic minority shopkeepers need special types of advice or special access to it (for example through literature in their own language); and identifying opportunities for and constraints on prevention.

As the report makes clear, due to the nature of the sample of shopkeepers obtained, the findings on crime and racial harassment can only provide the beginnings of a definitive picture of the problem, which appears to vary from one area to another. However, as intended, the picture obtained was sufficient as a basis for commenting on the scope for prevention, in particular indicating the need for those responsible for preventing crime and racially offensive incidents in a locality to develop, and act according to, a strategic view of the problem in their area, rather than confine themselves to individual casework. Perhaps the most important conclusion, though, is a general one: for Asian victims interviewed in this study crime and racial hostility overlapped, both in the actual experiences they reported, and the way these were perceived. Given that many keepers of small stores are Asians, all who are concerned with retail crime prevention should be aware of this special problem, and of the need to address it energetically as an integral part of any programme for crime prevention in small shops.

J A CHILCOT

Deputy Under Secretary of State
Home Office, Police Department
August 1988

Acknowledgements

We would like to thank staff of the Metroplitan Police Community Involvement Department, and the Crime Prevention Department of the Avon and Somerset Constabulary, for assistance provided in preparing for, and conducting the research; also Cris Tarrant and Sarah Molloy of NOP Ltd. for carrying out what was a methodologically rather challenging survey. We are grateful to the crime prevention officers who carried out a number of site inspections in London, and of course to the shopkeepers who readily gave the interviewers their time and attention. Colleagues in the Home Office and Dr. Robin Oakley of Brunel University provided useful comments and advice on the draft report. Finally, we are especially indebted to Sneh Birdi, who as sandwich student attached to the Crime Prevention Unit, was of great assistance in developing the project and piloting the interviews.

PAUL EKBLOM
FRANCES SIMON
August 1988

Contents

List of Tables

Introduction

Background

In 1985 the magazine *Independent Grocer* carried out an investigation into the kinds of crime suffered by shopkeepers in the grocery trade. Its report (Independent Grocer, 27 September and 11 October 1985) highlighted attacks and depredations suffered, particularly by Asians, and suggested that these shopkeepers were losing their faith in the ability of the police to prevent crime or to catch the perpetrators, and that their liaison with police crime prevention officers was poor. The *Independent Grocer's* survey occurred at a time of considerable interest in two related topics: racial attacks, a subject of continuing concern (as expressed earlier in a Home Office study (Home Office, 1981) and later by the House of Commons Home Affairs Committee (1986)); and crime prevention, which has received fresh Government emphasis and encouragement since 1984 (eg HO Circular 8/84).

Evidence by the Metropolitan Police to the Home Affairs Committee suggested that in London about 12% of the racial incidents reported to the police in 1985 occurred at places of business (HAC Third Report 1986, p.27). A pilot survey of 19 Asian shopkeepers in Walthamstow, carried out by the Home Office Crime Prevention Unit early in 1986, found that during a 12-month period almost half had been victims of assault, and similar proportions had suffered from window smashing, threats, and racial harassment. Discussions with the Metropolitan Police and with the Avon and Somerset Constabulary reinforced the view that in London and Bristol Asian shopkeepers were suffering from a considerable amount of crime. But little was systematically known of the extent to which crime suffered by business people is racially motivated. Indeed there appears to be almost no research into crimes suffered by businesses run by people of whatever race (Shapland and Vagg, 1985).

Crime in shops can occur in various ways. Opportunities for offending can be influenced by physical security equipment but also by shopkeepers' practices, including opening hours, the kinds of goods sold, the layout of shop furniture and displays, the handling of cash at the till, procedures like giving credit (which may affect the likelihood of disputes with customers), the number of shop staff and their social skills. It may be the case that ethnic minority retailers experience different patterns of 'ordinary' (eg purely materialistically-motivated) crime because they differ in terms of these practices, their clientele and the areas where the shops are located.

Racial attacks and abuse of shopkeepers may also arise in more than one way. They may be deliberate, perhaps pre-planned and racially motivated from the start. On the other hand, the racial component may emerge as a by-product of materially-motivated crime such as shop theft where an apprehended thief gives vent to racial abuse. In such a case the racism may be just as offensive to the shopkeeper, but measures to prevent future occurrences may be different. It also seems likely that problems faced by minority groups will vary from one locality to another, both objectively and subjectively.

1

Asians in a predominantly Asian community may feel more secure, and therefore perceive and respond to crime differently, compared with those working in areas that are predominantly West Indian or white.

These considerations have implications for crime prevention, and especially for the kinds of preventive advice offered to ethnic minority shopkeepers. So far, little attention has been paid to any ethnic dimension in official guidance on crime prevention, other than the translation into several languages of some leaflets addressed to the general public or to householders (not shopkeepers). To the extent that crime which is apparently racial has its origin in materialistic motivation, it may be susceptible to immediate preventive measures such as target-hardening, on which advice is already available — although ethnic minority business people may have special requirements for access to it. Deliberate and planned racial crime, however, may be preventible only by longer-term social measures (and by dealing with the offenders).

Aims of the present study

This study was intended to address some of these questions. Its original aims were:

(1) to describe the kinds of criminal and racial incidents suffered by small shopkeepers of different ethnic groups and in several different areas;

(2) to examine any relationships between these offences and particular characteristics of the shops;

(3) to record what preventive measures the shopkeepers took, and where they got preventive advice;

(4) to determine whether ethnic minority shopkeepers appeared to need special types of preventive advice or special access to advice; and

(5) to identify any constraints on prevention, such as costs.

The first of these aims had, however, to be modified because it was found that in the four areas selected for study so few keepers of small shops were not Asians that comparisons of different ethnic groups would be extremely difficult. To be set alongside 240 Asian shopkeepers, interviews were conducted with only 32 Whites and 20 Afro-Caribbeans. The main thrust of the study then became a description of the reported experiences of Asian shopkeepers in four areas, as a basis for considering issues in the prevention of crime and racially offensive behaviour in small retail stores.

Plan of the Study

In November 1986 NOP Market Research Ltd. carried out interviews with keepers of small retail stores in four parts of London. The areas were chosen because the centre of each includes numerous small shops run by people of ethnic minorities, and because in some other respects their populations differ from one another, thus forming a variety of settings in which the shopkeepers work.

The first area is centred on Muswell Hill, a mainly residential neighbourhood in the borough of Haringey. Though much of Haringey suffers from inner-city problems, Muswell Hill has retained its Edwardian air of a fashionable suburb, and the places immediately surrounding it, which include Highgate Wood and Alexandra Park, share its appearance of relative affluence. Thus the Asian shops serve a predominantly white middle-class area. When the interviewers were looking for suitable shops in which to seek interviews (see below) they began in Muswell Hill and spread out into surrounding neighbourhoods until they had found enough. The majority of interviews were in places which largely shared Muswell Hill's characteristics, though a minority were in poorer parts of Haringey. For convenience the whole area is referred to in this report as 'Muswell Hill', but it must be remembered that this label is not totally accurate.

The second area centres on Brixton in the borough of Lambeth. This district has a high concentration of residents of Afro-Caribbean descent, and relatively few Asians; its Asian shopkeepers thus work in a mainly black neighbourhood. Brixton is a commercial and residential district with relatively few owner-occupied houses, a history of severe social problems, and a high rate of recorded crime. The riots there in 1981 gave rise to the Scarman report (Scarman, 1981), and there was further disorder in 1985. For this survey the interviewers began in the immediate vicinity of Brixton station and spread out, collecting most of their sample in similar neighbourhoods but including a few in adjacent better-off areas to make up the numbers. Here the whole area is referred to as 'Brixton'.

The third area comprises mainly parts of the Borough of Brent. Brent is a centre of railways and engineering industry, but also has more owner-occupiers than the other three areas, and less recorded crime. It has the highest proportion of ethnic minority residents of all the London boroughs, with large numbers of both Afro-Caribbeans and Asians. Asian shopkeepers are therefore often close to many other Asian residents. Most of the shops selected for the survey were in two districts: one centred on Willesden where there is a high concentration of ethnic minorities, and the other located to the north of Brentwater where there are rather fewer. The whole area is described in the report as 'Brent'.

Finally, the fourth area is nearly all contained in the Borough of Newham. Newham has a large working-class population and is heavily industrialised, with miles of wharves and industries along the River Thames which forms its southern border. It was chosen for this study as an area where Asian shopkeepers would be largely surrounded by working-class whites, though in much of it there are as many Afro-Caribbean residents as Asians. In its evidence to the Home Affairs Committee on racial attacks in 1986, the Borough Council said (p.43):

"Newham faces some of the most deeply-rooted inner-city problems of any area of the country: high unemployment, serious housing problems, poor environment, low educational achievements, chronic social stress and racial disadvantage, and lack of adequate resources to tackle the problems . . . The 1970s saw a disturbing escalation of racial attacks in Newham. Newham has tended to provide fertile ground for the recruitment of National Front activists''.

The great majority of shopkeepers interviewed were in the neighbourhood of Stratford and parts immediately east as far as Upton Park. All are referred to here as being 'Newham'. Table A1.1[1] gives some statistics describing the contrasts between the four areas.

Shopkeepers were selected for interview first by the use of Kelly's Post Office Directory to pick out streets likely to contain shops, and then by the interviewers walking round them to identify shops meeting certain criteria described below. It had originally been intended to sample 30 white and 30 Asian shopkeepers in each area, plus 30 Afro-Caribbeans in Brixton. But the interviewers found that most of the small shops in the core of each area were Asian, so they first included as many white and Afro-Caribbeans as they could and then turned to Asians to make up the numbers. Altogether over 300 shopkeepers were approached, of whom 96% agreed to give an interview. The total was thus 296, comprising: Muswell Hill 61, Brixton 93, Brent 72, Newham 70. In each of these samples Asians were a large majority, from 69% in Brixton to 90% in Newham. The proportion of whites ranged between 7% in Newham and 18% in Muswell Hill. Only in Brixton was there an appreciable proportion of Afro-Caribbeans (19%); 18 of the 20 Afro-Caribbeans in the total sample were in Brixton. The overall result of this necessarily complex selection process was that what was originally intended to be a sample of small shopkeepers in each of four areas became something more closely akin to a survey of entire *populations* of small shopkeepers in each area — populations moreover, which were mainly Asian. All figures that follow relate to the 240 Asian shopkeepers only, unless otherwise stated. For interest, although not for comparison (since shopkeepers of different ethnic groups were not uniformly distributed across areas) the reported experiences of the white and black shopkeepers are summarised in Appendix 2.

The sample of shops was restricted to grocery/newsagent stores with not more than two service tills. Pure off-licences were not included, but stores with an off-licence component were. These selection criteria were intended to identify smaller stores (as opposed to supermarkets) of the 'corner shop' kind — which it was felt were perhaps more materially, economically and socially vulnerable to crime and racially-offensive behaviour than their larger counterparts. Nearly all the shops sold soft drinks, sweets, and tobacco; about half sold newspapers and magazines, and half sold food. Twenty-three per cent sold alcohol. Nine of the stores included sub-Post Office services.

---

(1) Tables numbered 'A1.1' etc are in Appendix 1.

The interviewers noted the location of the shops, trying to include as many as possible that were isolated from other shops, because they might be more vulnerable to crime. Only 27 of the 240 were classified as isolated in this way. The great majority were next to other shops, in a block or row in either the main shopping street or a side street.

Many of the shops were open for very long hours. On a weekday a quarter of them opened before 6.15 am, and over half were open by 8.15 am. The most likely closing time was around 7 pm, but a few stayed open till around 10 pm. Altogether nearly half of the shops were open for more than 12 hours on weekdays, and most opened on Sundays too, from early morning till part-way through the afternoon.

Most of the shops had just two staff working in them at any one time, and very few had more than three. Two-thirds of shopkeepers, asked to describe which ethnic groups their customers were drawn from, said ''a mixture''; nearly half in Muswell Hill (and fewer in Newham and Brent) said ''mostly white''; and one in five in Brixton said ''mostly African/West Indian''. No shop seemed to have just Asian customers.

All interviews were with shop owners or managers. There were four men respondents to every woman. Eighty-three percent owned their shops. The non-owners were usually members of the owner's family; fifty-six percent of the shopkeepers lived on the premises. Nearly all the shops were fully independent, the rest being franchisees or members of a chain.

The questions the shopkeepers were asked are listed in Appendix 4. The order and wording of questions were carefully designed to gain the interviewees' confidence, based on experience from the pilot study in Walthamstow. All interviews were carried out in the shop; if the respondent was not available or was too busy when first approached the interviewer made an appointment for another time. This was the most practical way of carrying out the interviews, but it is possible that some respondents' answers were influenced by the presence of other people in the shop.

All the interviewers were white[2]. Early in the study consideration was given to using ethnic minority interviewers, as had been done in the Walthamstow pilot. Advising against this, NOP referred to the ethnic diversity of the population to be sampled, and said, ''The ethnic groups identified are not homogeneous and it is virtually inevitable that an interviewer from one particular caste or sect would have to interview members of different groups as well as their own. Such interviewers are likely to meet much greater resistance from potential respondents than would the (stereo-) typical white, female, middle age, middle class interviewer who is the mainstay of all national fieldforces. It is well established that the latter are, overall, the least threatening to respondents and consequently the most likely to achieve the desired results''.

---

(2) Eleven interviewers were employed: 3 in Muswell Hill, 5 (of whom 1 did the majority) in Brixton, 2 in Brent and 1 in Newham.

NOP's own pilot interviews in North East London enabled comparison of the experience of a white and an Asian interviewer, and little difference was observed. In the main study, the 96% response rate obtained would seem to confirm this view. However, in terms of the *nature of respondents' answers*, from hindsight it must be said that some of the findings, especially those on crime and racial harassment reported by Asian shopkeepers in Newham, raise the question as to whether on some topics ethnic minority interviewers might have elicited more information. This is mentioned again later.

At the end of the interview shopkeepers were asked whether they would like a police crime prevention officer to visit and survey their premises, and if so, whether they would agree to the researchers seeing the officer's report. Those who said they would like a visit were given a card and stamped addressed enevlope to post to the appropriate police station, the Metropolitan Police having previously agreed with the researchers to carry out surveys for those who sent in cards. This resulted in the receipt of 31 completed survey forms (from shopkeepers of all ethnic groups), plus a note of 16 others done but not revealed at the shopkeeper's request. A few points arising from these 31 are included in this report.

Experiences of crime and other troubles

Worry about crime

Asked to say whether they worried about the risk of crime in and around their shops, the Asian shopkeepers answered as in Table 1.

Table 1: Asian shopkeepers' worry about the risk of crime

How much they worried	No.	%
A lot	50	21
A fair amount	57	24
A little	46	19
Not very much at all	41	17
Not worried	46	19
	240	100

Nearly two-thirds expressed some degree of worry. They were most worried in Newham, where 56% said they worried "a lot" or "a fair amount". Of those 154 shopkeepers (out of a total of 240) who worried a lot, a fair amount or a little, shop theft/stealing/pilfering was the problem of greatest concern (mentioned by over half the 154 respondents), followed by attacks, assaults and muggings (mentioned by a

6

third); around one in four mentioned burglary and robbery. There were clear differences between areas: 60% of the relevant Asians in Newham worried about attacks, assaults or mugging compared with 32% in Muswell Hill, 31% in Brixton and 8% in Brent. In Brixton nearly half the relevant shopkeepers (19 out of 39 of those who worried to some degree) felt there was a particular danger of hold-ups and robberies.

Many of those who worried about crime said they felt most at risk in the evening or after dark, though 20% said "any time" or "all the time". In Newham nearly three times as many shopkeepers as elsewhere said they worried all the time or at any time (17 out of 48 of those who worried to some degree).

Shopkeepers who worried about crime were asked whether there were any particular local sources of trouble for the shop that concerned them. Three-quarters answered "no". Among those in Newham, 94% answered "no". It seems that although the Newham Asians worried most about crime, particularly attacks, they were not able (or willing) to tell the interviewer of any specific local reasons related to the shop.

Experiences of crime

Crime surveys (eg Hough and Mayhew, 1985) normally note each individual incident within a fixed recall period (eg 12 months), but this was not appropriate here as shopkeepers suffered high rates of some offences and could not recall individual incidents. In asking the Asian shopkeepers whether they or their staff had suffered any of a list of crimes and other incidents, it was decided to give them a range of alternative responses from 'ever suffered (eg) assault' to 'daily suffered assault'. Table 2 presents the results.

The frequency of crime

Altogether, four-fifths of the shopkeepers said they had ever experienced one or more of these kinds of crime or incident. The most prevalent[3] was shop theft, which over half of all the shopkeepers had ever experienced; the next most prevalent were window smashing, threatening behaviour, verbal abuse and snatches from the till, each of which a quarter or more said they had suffered. One in seven had experienced assault. The rarest were abusive literature, arson, and theft by shop staff (and no murders were reported).

Considering the overall pattern in the table, for each offence there is a wide variation of rates between individual shopkeepers — for example, some suffered threatening behaviour daily, others only weekly, monthly or yearly. Some shopkeepers suffered

---

(3) In studying experiences of crime a distinction is to be made between *prevalence* (the number of shopkeepers victimised one or more times within a given period) and *incidence* (the total number of crimes reported as occurring within the period) (see Bottoms, Mawby and Walker, 1987).

some types of offence very frequently indeed: 28 reported theft as a daily occurrence, 9 reported threatening behaviour weekly, and 13 reported verbal abuse daily.

Table 2: Asian shopkeepers' experience of particular crimes and other incidents

Total No. of shopkeepers	**240**						
Those who said they had suffered:	ever	% ever	less than yearly	a few times a year	monthly	weekly	daily
arson, fire raising	3	1	—	—	—	—	—
snatch from the till	57	24	44	11	1	—	—
price switching	20	8	4	8	5	2	1
theft of goods, shoplifting	130	54	4	39	23	35	28
cheque/credit card fraud	43	18	18	19	4	1	—
threatening behaviour	66	28	17	25	11	9	3
assault	34	14	22	9	—	2	—
theft by shop staff	4	2	2	2	—	—	—
murder	—	—	—	—	—	—	—
robbery	40	17	33	5	1	—	—
window smashing	80	33	68	9	2	1	—
graffiti	24	10	14	5	3	1	1
other damage	14	6	7	4	2	1	—
disputes with customers over:							
charging/change	21	9	2	10	4	4	1
credit	17	7	3	4	4	1	5
returned goods	13	5	2	5	4	2	—
verbal abuse	65	27	9	30	6	7	13
abusive phone calls	19	8	5	9	3	—	2
abusive/offensive letters/literature	—	—	—	—	—	—	—
none of these	48	20					

Burglary was not included in the questionnaire at this stage but incidence rates were calculated from later questions, and these are discussed on pages (p.13)[4].

Crime by area

As only fifty to sixty Asian shopkeepers were interviewed in each area, comparisons for individual offences are based on small numbers, although they do represent a large part of the Asian small shopkeeper population in those areas. The results are presented

(4) This postponement of the burglary questions may have served to increase the recall or admission rate relative to the other crimes because the shopkeepers may have been more at ease with the interviewer by that time, or the more detailed questions encouraged them to say more.

in Table 3. Their main use in the current context though is simply to demonstrate the wide variation between areas in the prevalence of particular crimes and related incidents. Till snatch, for example, appears more than twice as prevalent in Brixton as in Brent or Newham; shop theft appears less than half as prevalent in Newham as elsewhere; threats are about twice as prevalent in Muswell Hill and Brixton as in Brent and Newham. Robbery is over twice as prevalent in Brixton as anywhere else in the survey.

Table 3: Asian shopkeepers' experience of crime and other incidents, by area

Total No. of shopkeepers	Muswell Hill		Brixton		Brent		Newham	
	49		64		64		63	
Those who said they had ever suffered:	No.	%	No.	%	No.	%	No.	%
arson	1	(2)	1	2	1	2	—	—
till snatch	12	(24)	25	39	10	16	10	16
price switch	6	(12)	9	14	4	6	1	2
shoplifting	35	(71)	43	67	37	58	15	24
fraud	8	(16)	18	28	17	27	—	—
threats	17	(35)	26	41	13	20	10	16
assault	7	(14)	16	25	3	5	8	13
theft by staff	2	(4)	—	—	2	3	—	—
robbery	3	(6)	22	34	6	9	9	14
window smashing	23	(47)	18	28	24	38	15	24
graffiti	9	(18)	8	13	6	9	1	2
other damage	1	(2)	8	13	3	5	2	3
disputes over:								
charging/change	6	(12)	7	11	5	8	3	5
credit	7	(14)	7	11	3	5	—	—
returned goods	3	(6)	6	9	4	6	—	—
verbal abuse	14	(29)	24	38	11	17	16	25
abusive phone calls	7	(14)	7	11	5	8	—	—
none of these	6	(12)	7	11	10	16	25	40

Note: percentages in brackets derive from bases where 100% is less than 50 respondents.

Considering the four areas overall, Newham was apparently the safest, a surprising result in view of its reputation for racial hostility: 40% of the Asian shopkeepers there said they had never experienced any of the crimes or incidents listed (a figure which, it must be said of shop theft at least, strains credibility and suggests reticence on the part of the shopkeepers there). The worst areas were Brixton and Muswell Hill where only 11% and 12% respectively said they had not been victims; in Brent the proportion was 16%. Muswell Hill seemed to be the worst area for shop theft, window smashing

9

and graffiti, while till snatch and robbery seemed most frequent in Brixton. However, in considering these figures it must be remembered that the study areas of Muswell Hill and Brixton extended beyond the immediate neighbourhoods suggested by their names.

The greater worry about crime among Asian shopkeepers in Newham, compared with the other areas, contrasted with their reported experiences. Table 3 lists 17 kinds of incident; for 12 of these, including threats and window smashing, there were fewer Asian victims in Newham than in any of the other three areas, and none of the 17 was commonest in Newham. Estimates of incidence rates for burglary again suggested Newham as having the lowest; for assault the rate was near the average (Tables A1.2, A1.3 and A1.4). The victimisation rates for Newham Asians are discussed in the final section of this report.

Crime by type and site of shop

A number of relationships emerged between reported crime and the type and site of shop. Shops selling alcohol seemed more likely than others to suffer from cheque frauds and disputes over credit. The few sub-post offices had attracted a disproportionate number of threats and robberies, though for them shop thefts, frauds, and till snatches were rare. Shops in side streets had suffered more than others from till snatches, threats and graffiti. Since the distribution of the site of shops varied between areas (with Newham having a preponderance of shops located in rows in main streets, Brixton shops in rows in side streets and Brent in main shopping areas in main streets) it is not possible with the small numbers here to disentangle effects of the immediate site from effects of the wider area.

Racial motivation of crimes

Defining racially-motivated crime is a very difficult matter, involving consideration of the race of offender and victim, the offender's intentions, and the victim's perceptions. The Association of Chief Police Officers, having wrestled with the question, issued a working definition in January 1986 as follows: "A racial attack is any incident in which it appears to the reporting or investigating officer that the complaint involves an element of racial motivation, or any incident which includes an allegation of racial motivation made by any person". This is a subjective assessment. It has the merit of taking full account of the perceptions of the victim, but to be properly understood these should be placed in the context of the experiences of the victim's ethnic group within the total community, including power relationships with other residents and organisations (for example if the victims belong to an ethnic minority group whose members in the locality are relatively sparse and/or scattered, their perception of vulnerability and the fact of vulnerability may be greater than if they were more densely settled). The present study adopted the simple method of accepting victims' accounts of their experiences, though the context for Asians in Newham is discussed in Appendix 3.

The particular approach employed was twofold. First, for each of the types of crime or incident covered in the study, victims were asked what proportion of the incidents they had experienced they felt were racially motivated. The results of this are shown in Table 4. The second approach, discussed later, involved asking respondents specifically and in some detail about explicit acts of racial harassment.

Table 4: Victims of crimes and other incidents: attribution of racial motives

Type of crime or incident	No. of Asian shopkeepers who had ever suffered	No. of those victims thinking at least some incidents were racially motivated	%
arson	3	2	(67)
till snatch	57	12	21
price switch	20	1	(5)
shoplifting	130	12	9
fraud	43	2	(5)
threats	66	24	36
assaults	34	15	(44)
theft by staff	4	—	(0)
robbery	40	6	(15)
window smashing	80	14	18
graffiti	24	9	(38)
other damage	14	2	(14)
disputes over:			
charging/change	21	5	(20)
credit	17	1	(6)
returned goods	13	1	(8)
verbal abuse	65	22	34
abusive phone calls	19	11	(58)

Note: percentages in brackets derive from bases where 100% is less than 50 respondents.

Some offence types were more likely to be thought racially motivated as the right hand column in the table shows: arson, verbal and telephone abuse, assault, threats and graffiti. Others were less likely to be seen this way: price switching, shop theft, fraud, staff theft, and robbery. On the face of it, the divide appears to be along the distinction between 'expressive' and 'instrumental or materialistic' offences, which one might have expected. There are however important qualifications. First, in virtually every offence type *some* victims perceived racial motivation — even with what might be considered highly materialistic crimes such as shop theft or till snatch. Second, with the expressive offences (with the exception of arson — only 3 cases in all — and abusive phone calls), in no incident type does the proportion of victims perceiving racial motivation exceed 50%. There is then a considerable overlap in perceived motivation — a substantial number of materialistic crimes may involve racial motivation while a substantial number of expressive ones may be thought not to. With the possible exception of arguments over change and charging, disputes were relatively rarely seen as racially motivated.

Considering the different areas, victims in Newham were generally more likely to attribute racial motives for crimes than those elsewhere, and this was specially true for till snatches and shop theft even though in fact fewer shopkeepers in Newham said they had suffered these things: among shop theft victims, 10 of the 15 Newham shopkeepers suspected some racial motivation whereas only two of all the other 115 shopkeepers did. Threats and verbal abuse were attributed to racial motives by slightly more shopkeepers in Brixton than in other areas, and more Brixton shopkeepers had been victims of these. Racial motives were least often attributed by those in Brent.

The extent to which victims thought crimes racially inspired did not seem strongly related to particular characteristics of their shops, although threats, window smashing, and verbal abuse were more often racially attributed by people whose shops were comparatively isolated, who did not open very early, and who did not live on the premises.

Consequences for business

Victims were asked which, if any, of the crimes they had suffered they considered to be serious problems for the long-term running and future of their business. Only a small minority said there were serious problems, and only for some types of crime. This included eight of the 40 robbery victims, and smaller proportions of the victims of till snatch, shop theft, assault and verbal abuse. Sub-postmasters mentioned problems more often than other shopkeepers.

Reporting crime to the police

Sixty-two percent of shopkeepers said they would always or quite often report crimes to the police (Table 5). There was marked variation by area. Shopkeepers in Newham and Brent were more likely to say they would report always or quite often (79% and 78%) than those in Muswell Hill and Brixton (49% and 46%). Shopkeepers in isolated locations more often said they would report.

Nearly all who said "it depends" implied that they would report the incident if they thought it serious enough. When those who said they would not often or never report were asked why not, 33 out of the relevant 60 shopkeepers gave answers like "not serious, not worth bothering about"; only eight said "it's a waste of time, police never do anything", etc. This suggests that the majority of shopkeepers had some faith in the police, in that they were prepared to report most of the crimes they suffered; and that while some felt it was a waste of time because the police would not respond, a larger number were confident of dealing with at least minor incidents themselves.

Table 5: Whether victims said they would report crimes to the police

Those who said they would report	No.	%
always/quite often	119	62
not very often/never	60	31
it depends	10	5
other answers	3	2%
	192	100

Burglary, assault and racial harassment

Later in the interview the shopkeepers were asked whether in the last 12 months they or their staff had suffered from any of three specified crimes: burglary, assault, or racial harassment. Those who had were asked for details of the most recent occurrence.

Burglary

Fifty-two shopkeepers (22%) said they had suffered a burglary (or attempted burglary) at their shop within the past year. The numbers were highest in Muswell Hill and Brent, where nearly a third said they had been burgled, and lowest in Newham (13%).

Victims were asked when the most recent burglary (or attempt) had occurred. Sixteen had been burgled within the last three months, including seven within the last month. When estimates of annual incidence were calculated it appeared that on average the shopkeepers were likely to suffer a burglary once every four years (Table A1.2). The estimated incidence was highest in Brent and lowest in Newham (Table A1.4).

Describing the most recent incident, about half the 52 victims said the burglars had got in, or tried to get in, by breaking parts of the building: mainly windows, doors or locks. In five cases grilles or shutters had been broken or bent. In three cases the burglars had entered through residential quarters or neighbouring premises.

Six shopkeepers said the offenders had threatened them with weapons and demanded money from the till: in four cases the criminals had carried guns, and in three, knives. One victim had been hit with a bottle. One had lost £3,000 worth of stock[5].

---

(5) These cases would normally be classified as robbery or aggravated burglary.

Forty victims said they had reported the burglary to the police, four did not know whether it had been reported, and eight had not reported it. Some of the latter said it was because the police already knew, but three gave answers implying lack of confidence in the police. One of them said, "If you report it they come two days later".

Asked whether they knew anything about the people who carried out the burglaries, 16 victims said they did. The descriptions given by this small group built up a picture of the burglars as being nearly all young men (between about 16 and 25 years old), acting singly, or in twos and threes. Seven of the victims said the burglars were white and six said they were West Indian/African; none were said to be Asian. Most of the 52 victims thought the burglars had acted for material gain. Only four (including just one in Newham) thought that there might have been any racial motivation, and only one of them mentioned it unprompted as the main reason. Asked why they thought their shop had been picked rather than others, many said they did not know and others suggested vulnerable features of the shop or goods which might attract burglars. Ten victims thought it was not just their shop — "all shops are getting done"; this in fact was the most frequent response other than "don't know".

Assault

Twenty-eight shopkeepers (12%) said that they or their staff had been assaulted in the past 12 months, not counting assaults linked to burglaries. Victimisations were most frequent in Brixton (17%) and lowest in Brent (6%). About half the occurrences had been within the last three months. When incidence estimates were calculated as for burglaries, the figure was about once in eight years (Table A1.3). It was highest in Brixton and lowest in Brent (Table A1.4).

Half the victims had not been injured, but one had suffered serious injuiries. In at least six cases weapons had been used, including knives and an axe. Half the assaults had occurred in furtherance of crime, including snatches from the till, or had happened when the shopkeeper tried to deal with thefts or disorder in the shop. A quarter (seven) had arisen in dispute with customers over matters like refusal of credit or refusal to cash giro cheques. A few of the victims could suggest no motive, and a few did not think their shop in particular had been picked on. Seven victims thought there had definitely or possibly been a racial motive. Three of these victims mentioned racially abusive language by the offenders, and one other said he knew his attackers from past similar experience. Four of these seven victims were in Brixton and one in each of the other three areas.

Twenty victims were able to give some description of their assailants. Nearly all were men, mainly young though a few were over 35, and most had acted in company rather than alone. Ten victims identified assailants as white and 13 as West Indian/African; no assailants were said to be Asian.

14

Twenty-one victims, including all eight in Newham, had reported the assault to the police. Among the seven who had not, three said it was because the incident was only minor; only one said calling the police was a waste of time.

Racial harassment

It is not easy, when interviewing shopkeepers or when writing about the results, to draw a distinction between racial *motivation* as a component of apparently materialistic crimes and racial *harassment* as the predominant, explicit and deliberate motive behind an attack on shopkeepers and their property. Both are worthy of serious concern. Nonetheless it was felt the term 'harassment' has sufficient currency, and refers to a sufficiently distinguishable set of acts, for an attempt to cover it as a separate issue.

Altogether 20 Asian shopkeepers (8% of those interviewed) said that in the past 12 months they had been victims of racial harassment. Half said this had been a single incident and half said a series. The proportion of victims was highest in Brixton and Muswell Hill, and lowest in Newham, only 3% of Newham Asians reporting racial harassment.

Asked to describe the harassment, most victims referred to verbal abuse extending sometimes to swearing and shouting. Ten did not say what, if anything, had prompted this, but others offered reasons: "Youngsters with nothing to occupy their minds, they get jealous and shout abuse". Four respondents described shop disputes or purchasing mistakes in which frustrated customers gave vent to racial insults. "Someone bought the wrong ticket and called all Indians thieves". In another case a customer's retaliation had been delayed; "Someone was cutting papers, I caught him and told him to stop — he came in one morning and hit me, knocked a tooth out".

In a few cases the harassment was clearly planned and deliberate. "Some boys pick up a tin and say 'we'll pay next time' — and we're scared to challenge them in case of attack". "They try to pick a fight, asking 'why are you here?'". Two victims — both in Muswell Hill — had had their shops defaced by National Front posters or graffiti.

Thirteen victims, including all nine in Brixton, said they knew something about the people who harassed them. Most were young men, but about a third were women and a third were over 35. Most acted alone. Eight victims said there were white offenders and seven said that West Indians/Africans were involved; none were said to be Asian.

Only three of the 20 victims had reported the matter to the police. Most who had not reported gave reasons implying that they did not think the matter serious enough, but seven said that the police could not or would not do anything about it. One said, "if we report it we'd get in even more trouble". Four victims said it was a routine occurrence. There were no differences between areas in these answers.

Crime prevention and insurance

Preventive measures

The shopkeepers were shown a list of possible measures to prevent crime and were asked which if any, they took. (Their answers are shown in Table A1.5.) Measures concerning shop layout — the placing of shelves, gondolas, tills and counters — were common. Very few shopkeepers said they employed extra staff to prevent trouble, or kept certain customers out, and few restricted opening hours. But nearly a third said they watched certain individuals or types of customers closely. About one in eight said they followed practices aimed at avoiding or reducing disputes. Many said they took special care when cashing up.

Among technological methods the commonest were grilles or shutters, and mirrors, used by about two-thirds, and then burglar alarms (53%), security door locks (49%) and security window locks (33%). About one in six people had protected letter boxes. Video cameras were rare, and so were dummy cameras and alarms.

Very few put up deterrent notices (eg "Shoplifting is Theft"). About a sixth kept dogs. Most kinds of preventive measures did not appear to differ much between the four areas, or between shops of different types. Shops selling alcohol were generally more security conscious. Shopkeepers in Newham paid more attention than those elsewhere to features of shop layout, and took more care when cashing up. Isolated shopkeepers also took more care when cashing up while those on main streets and main shopping areas were generally more relaxed about security. Weapons for personal defence were very rare, except among shopkeepers in Brixton of whom one in eight had them.

Asked whether there were any difficulties that had deterred them from adopting crime prevention measures, 88% of the shopkeepers could not think of any. Only 11 said they had been put off by the cost. Four people said they were all right as they were.

Shopkeepers who had been victims of burglary, assault, or racial harassment in the past year were asked if they were taking any steps to prevent it from happening again. Most burglary victims said they were doing something, the commonest specific measures being installation or upgrading of existing shutters, locks, alarms and doors — all instances of target hardening. By contrast, nine of the 28 shopkeepers who had been assaulted said they were trying to prevent repetition by personal deameanor (eg being more watchful or avoiding arguments). Only one had taken on extra staff; a quarter felt there was nothing they could do. Half of the 20 victims of racial harassment felt there was nothing they could do; but several said they were trying to avoid further trouble, by "being nice", "being subtle", or ignoring taunts.

16

Insurance

The great majority of shopkeepers (80%) said they were insured against criminal activity. Asked what types of crime they were insured against, some said "everything" or "all the usual", but many gave specific answers (see Table A1.6 for details). The crime most often specified was assault or injury to staff, against which 43% were insured; next came theft (37%) damage or vandalism (26%) and fire/arson (20%). Burglary was mentioned by only 18%.

The four areas showed some interesting differences. In Muswell Hill and Brent at least 95% of shopkeepers were insured, nearly two-thirds of them specifying theft and, in Muswell Hill, vandalism; the numbers mentioning assault were noticeably smaller. In Newham, shopkeepers were less likely to be insured than elsewhere for almost every type of risk except assault. Fifty-six percent of the Newham Asians said they were covered against assault, whereas only 6% or fewer specified other types of crime; 30% said they did not know whether their shops were insured. In Brixton three times as many shopkeepers as elsewhere said they were insured against robbery.

Three of the 20 who were not insured said that companies had refused them. All these shopkeepers were in Brixton, and some mentioned the riots. Four people (from all areas combined) said they could not afford insurance, and five felt they did not need it; there were no reliable area differences in these answers. Shopkeepers who had suffered burglary, assault, or racial harassment in the past year were asked whether, before it happened, they had been insured against it, and if so, whether they had claimed and with what results. Forty-six of the 52 burglary victims had been insured, and 28 of these had made a claim. Most claimants had the bulk of their loss met, but seven fared less well: five received only half the amount claimed, one got a quarter, and one had his claim rejected. Of the 28 assault victims 12 said they had been insured but only one had claimed (and had received payment). None of the victims of racial harassment said they had been insured against its effects.

The 193 shopkeepers who carried any insurance cover were asked whether its requirements had influenced any of their crime prevention measures. Two-thirds said it had not. One in five had been persuaded to install alarms (burglar or attack), and smaller numbers had installed shutters, grilles, special locks or other target-hardening devices. More than half the 56 people who had taken such measures said they had cost more than £1,000 to install, and none had cost under £100. Nearly half of those who had installed devices paid annual running costs of more than £100.

Advice on crime prevention

The majority of shopkeepers (81%) said they had not received advice on crime prevention from anyone. Those who had had nearly all been advised by the police; other advisers, such as insurers, security companies, or fellow shopkeepers were rarely mentioned. The great majority of those who had received advice said they had been satisfied with it.

Part-way through the interview, those people who had not received crime prevention advice from the police were aksed whether that was something they would like to have, and if so, whether they would prefer a visit from a police crime prevention officer or to receive leaflets. Two-thirds said they would like advice, with about equal numbers opting for a visit and for leaflets (and a few said they would like both). But this pattern was different among the shopkeepers in Newham, where although 71% said they would like advice most wanted it only by leaflets, and (in contrast to those elsewhere who said leaflets) most wanted then written in an Asian language.

At the end of the interview the subject was raised again, with more detail and explanation of what would be involved. All the shopkeepers were asked if they would be interested in receiving a visit from a police or crime prevention officer in the next few weeks, to carry out a free survey of their premises and recommend appropriate measures. The interviewer said that none of their previous interview answers would be passed onto the police, although the researchers would like to see the officers report without the shopkeeper being identified to them. One hundred and forty-eight (62%) told the interviewer they would like a visit; the proportion saying yes was highest among shopkeepers in Newham (71%).

However, in the event only 31 completed survey forms were available to the researchers (from shopkeepers of *all* ethnic groups, pooled because of small numbers and missing ethnic information on the forms); this suggests that some respondents had second thoughts about wanting a visit, though some forms were not available for other reasons. Information from the 31 may not be typical, and also crime prevention officers' survey methods and preferences may vary. In the majority of these 31 cases the officer thought the level of security was reasonably good, but nevertheless 24 shopkeepers were advised to make improvements. The advice most often given was about cash in the till: 16 shopkeepers were reminded of the importance of keeping the cash level low, banking regularly, and not taking the money home. Several were advised to fit a small wall safe, costing around £200, in which to keep the cash between bank trips. Other recommendations included strengthening parts of the building, re-positioning displays, and making other changes in practice. One shopkeeper was advised not to keep a minder unless he was employed by a known security firm. In only one case did the estimated cost of the recommended measures exceed £300.

Discussion

Methodological issues

This study involved investigating the amount and kinds of crime and offensive incidents suffered by Asian shopkeepers of small retail stores in four different areas of London, according to the answers they gave to NOP interviewers in late 1986. An original intention had been to gather equal samples of Asian and white shopkeepers in all the areas, and of Afro-Caribbeans in one, and to compare the ethnic groups.

However it was found that in all four areas (which had been chosen partly for having high numbers of ethnic minority residents) the great majority of small retail shops were run by Asians, so reliable and representative comparisons were not possible.

Generalisation to the situation of Asian shopkeepers elsewhere in the country (for example to establish nationally representative incidence rates for particular offences in the manner of the British Crime Survey) is also difficult, as it was not possible to set up a random sampling process of individual shopkeepers. Instead, the method more closely resembled a non-random sampling of four areas chosen to provide a variety of social contexts, within each of which a large part of the population of Asian shopkeepers was interviewed. The study was not, therefore, a crime survey in the usual sense. The information on crime and other offensive behaviour experienced by the Asian shopkeepers was intended to be a guide to the scope for prevention, and the findings are discussed below in this restricted context.

One final qualification is worth repeating here. The decision to opt for conventional white interviewers may have had some effect on the kind of responses obtained from the Asian shopkeepers (although it cannot have served to reduce the overall response rate, which was extremely high) but for reasons outlined in the introduction this issue remains unresolved.

Experience of crime and racially offensive behaviour

Overall, it seemed that these small shops were the focus of a considerable amount of crime. More than four out of five interviewees said they had experienced some sort of crime at their shops — most often theft, but also burglary, assault, window smashing, threatening behaviour, and other kinds. While some incidents were minor and in general did not seem to constitute a serious problem for business, others were destructive, expensive and frightening.

Simply to give an impression of the scale of the problem in these four areas, it is possible very roughly to compare the risk rates for burglary and assault with those reported by private individuals through the British Crime Survey in 1983. During the past year one in four Asian shopkeepers had been burgled (including attempts) one or more times. This proportion is about twice as high as the proportion of householders in high-risk areas (multi-racial areas and the poorest council estates) who told interviewers for the British Crime Survey that they had suffered burglary in 1983 (Hough and Mayhew, 1985). Even allowing for a three-year difference, and for possibly different interpretations of burglary by some interviewees, it seems very likely that Asian shopkeepers were more at risk than private residents in some areas. Estimation of the rate of incidence from the shopkeepers' answers suggested that their annual chances of burglary might be about one in four. For assaults, the annual rate of incidence was estimated at about one in eight. This risk is comparable to that suggested by the British Crime Survey for residents of multiracial areas, though much higher than for the population as a whole[6].

When asked specifically about racial harassment, one in twelve shopkeepers said they had suffered some in the past twelve months. But for virtually every kind of crime or offensive behaviour experienced, a proportion of shopkeepers (ranging from 1 in 20 to 2 out of 3) saw at least some of the incidents as racially motivated. Worry about crime may, as with householders, show a different pattern from actual victimisation and may be dependent on wider contextual factors such as insecurity in the face of racial hostility experienced by shopkeepers in their role as private residents (on the street, in the home) rather than in the course of running a shop. The figures for shopkeepers in Brent, with a relatively high Asian population, suggested some contrasts with Asians elsewhere. The Brent Asians reported fewer incidents of assault (though not other crimes), were less worried about the risk of attacks (though not about other crimes) and were less inclined to attribute crime to racial motives.

The discrepancy between worry and actual experience — as reported — is striking in the case of Asian shopkeepers in Newham. Their level of worry was higher than that of Asian shopkeepers elsewhere, and they were more likely to attribute crime to racial motives and to insure themselves against assault (though little else). Yet according to their interview answers they actually suffered the lowest rates for crimes generally, and for burglary and racial harassment in particular. Only three percent reported racial harassment, although racial motivation was attributed to many of the other offences suffered — and they were more likely than those in the other areas to attribute racial motivation to 'materialistic' crimes such as shop theft and till snatches. Ninety-four percent could give the interviewer no specific reasons, connected with the shop, for their worries about crime. Possible reasons for this discrepancy between stated levels of worry and stated levels of crime, and the futher discrepancy between present crime levels and those found by the Newham crime survey, are discussed in Appendix 3; for the present, it should be noted that the absolute crime levels described by Asian shopkeepers in Newham should not be taken at face value.

The current state of prevention

Measures that Asian shopkeepers took to prevent crime seemed to be generally in line with the risks they faced, and with the kinds of advice given in the Home Office booklet *Profit from Prevention,* which is designed to help those in charge of small shops prevent theft, burglary and robbery. Many shopkeepers had spent much money on target-hardening measures, sometimes, but by no means always, at the request of their insurers. There was little evidence in the study that insurers were

---

(6) Table B in Hough and Mayhew (1985) estimates the rate for the population aged 16 plus as about 1 in 20. This is for all areas; if in multi-racial areas it is higher by the same factor as is suggested by Table A1.2 on the prevalence of burglaries, the estimated incidence becomes about 1 in 7.

making unreasonable demands (as the pilot work suggested might be happening). But five percent of the shopkeepers said they had been put off preventive measures by the cost, and a small number (under two percent) felt they could not afford insurance; the interviews did not explore these matters further. In addition, another one percent were handicapped by being refused insurance because they were in a high-risk area — the proportion amounting to 3 out of 64 in that area. This, and the fact that in the same area 12% kept weapons for personal defence, is cause for concern.

Crime prevention measures recommended by the police (in the 31 CPO surveys reported, for all ethnic groups) were generally less expensive than those which insurers had requested, but of course there is no direct comparison because the more expensive ones may have already been in place. The advice often given by CPOs to keep the till cash level low, bank regularly and fit a wall safe seemed apposite in view of the frequency with which shopkeepers mentioned experience of, or worry about, till snatches and hold-ups.

Implications for prevention

The pattern of victimisation revealed by the shopkeepers has important implications for preventive strategy. A number of points can be made which draw on the findings in more detail.

(1)   Frequencies of offending within some individual shops are high enough to establish patterns of offending there, on the basis of which fairly specific strategies can be tailor-made (as in larger stores — see Ekblom, 1986; Burrows, 1988). In view of the difficulties shopkeepers had in keeping track of say, shop theft, they should be encouraged to keep a log of incidents detailing time of incident, location within shop, goods stolen, method of offence, associated dispute etc. This log could be initiated with the help of a police crime prevention officer (CPO) who could then return after a month or two to examine its contents.

(2)   Some shops appear much harder-hit than others for various offences. CPOs could give priority to aiding these, but in order to do this, they would need to have a working knowledge of the average levels of crime suffered by shopkeepers in their area. Isolated shops seem somewhat more prone to trouble and could perhaps be targeted in the absence of such knowledge, as could shops selling alcohol, where specific advice could be developed eg on handling of credit.

(3)   Patterns of crime differed between the four areas. In spite of shopkeepers' worries (see below) Newham appeared in some respects to be the safest area; Muswell Hill had the highest rates of shop theft, threats, window smashing and graffiti, while till snatch and robbery were most frequent in Brixton (where some shopkeepers had been refused insurance and a few kept weapons for personal protection). This variation suggests the importance of developing a strategic view of prevention in a locality, rather than the sole pursuit of the demand-led, one-at-a-time visits involved in casework.

(4)   The apparent mismatch between worry about shop crime and actual levels of victimisation in an area suggests that worry, and its relationship with general insecurity about racial hostility, should be taken account of as a factor in its own right in strategic planning of preventive (and supportive) measures.

(5)   A third of shopkeepers said they never or not very often reported crimes suffered to the police, although the decision not to report appeared to derive much more from a belief that not much could be achieved, than by any antipathy to the police. The proportion of offences reported to the police varied noticeably by area, and from shopkeeper to shopkeeper. These findings suggest that the pattern of incidents shown in police crime reports alone may be an inadequate basis for devising local preventive strategies; this information should be supplemented by some kind of survey, or less formal equivalent, although in parallel there is value in effort to increase the proportion of crimes and racially offensive incidents reported by members of ethnic minorities to the police.

(6)   Four out of five shopkeepers had not received preventive advice from any source, but two-thirds of these said they would be pleased to receive it, suggesting that demand-led work by CPOs be supplemented by proactive offering of services. This could be done through leaflets as well as visits. Leaflets and visits were favoured by equal numbers of shopkeepers; in three areas English language leaflets were acceptable whilst Newham shopkeepers opted for Asian language ones, implying again that a strategic knowledge of the requirements of the locality is useful.

(7)   The high rate of offences experienced, together with the racial nature of a significant proportion, would appear to justify extra effort, whether in identifying the nature and extent of local problems, or in 'outreach' work where CPOs initiated contact with shopkeepers through visits or leaflets. One example of such outreach work occurred in a racially sensitive part of Bristol during episodes of public disorder. CPOs took the initiative in calling on ethnic minority business people to offer guidance on protecting their premises against the possibility of damage, and gave them details of suppliers of equipment, price lists etc. These visits were well-received and contributed to general improvements in communication between the police and ethnic minorities.

(8)   While offences normally considered materialistic were less likely to be judged by shopkeepers to involve racial motivation than were 'expressive' crimes such as assault or window breaking, the divide was by no means clearcut. Even with such apparently materialistically-motivated offences as shop theft or till snatch, some victims perceived racial motivation, suggesting that those responsible for prevention should constantly be alert to the racial dimension. As with shop theft in Newham, this relationship may be stronger in some areas than others, again indicating the need to establish a local strategic understanding.

(9)   Similarly, the expressive crimes were less frequently ascribed to racial motives than to other causes such as furtherance of material crime or a consequence of dispute. While racial motivation remains a strong possibility more conventional avenues of prevention should not be neglected.

(10)   Detailed questioning on incidents of racial harassment suggested that not all such cases involved deliberate planning by the perpetrator — shop disputes and purchasing mistakes had sometimes triggered off racial abuse. It would therefore seem that some scope exists for reducing some aspects of racial harassment by restricting the opportunity for materialistic crime and by making changes in general shop practices aimed at reducing disputes and mistakes (for example clear, consistent and well-advertised policies over credit, payment by cheque, returned goods etc; and bill/change giving procedures).

With the exception of the racial hostility problem, many of the possibilities discussed above could equally apply to shopkeepers of all ethnic groups. And many of the suggestions slanted towards the work of police CPOs could be equally relevant to other agencies — official, private or voluntary — with a role in reducing crime or racial hostility (and one would hope a coordinated approach could be achieved, for example between local authority departments, ethnic minority welfare groups, retailers' associations and the police crime prevention/community relations branches). Action at a national level could include broadening the scope of *Profit from Prevention* to include advice on avoiding or containing disputes, dealing with awkward customers and minimising the chances of property crimes turning into assaults[6].

Some shopkeepers appeared to have evolved ways to reduce both assaults and racial harassment, by being watchful, avoiding arguments and ignoring taunts. A set of people regularly exposed in their working life to crime and offensive incidents surely have as much practical knowledge to contribute as the professionals, in terms of procedural means of prevention and those relying on social skills, as well as their experience of target-hardening tactics — but it needs to be drawn together for all to use, and refined. At the local level there is a role here for self-help within business groups such as chambers of commerce, shopping street associations, Business Watch schemes or fellow franchisees, in clarifying local problems, obtaining advice, and developing and implementing solutions. Collective action may be especially valuable for shopkeepers whose premises are isolated. At the national level the development of a body of advice could usefully involve tapping shopkeepers' wisdom in some kind of working group; perhaps even an action/demonstration project involving a local group of keepers of small retail stores acting in collaboration with CPOs.

Summary of recommendations

(a)   Crime suffered by Asian keepers of small shops (and, probably, those in all

---

(6) For examples of practical advice in a somewhat similar field, see *The Prevention of Violence Associated with Licensed Premises* (report of the Working Group): Home Office, 1986.

ethnic groups) is a problem worthy of attention; the racially-offensive behaviour associated with it further heightens its significance. Fear of shop crime may in some areas be a problem worth tackling in its own right.

(b)   CPOs and others addressing the problem might adopt a strategic view, setting shop crime and racially offensive behaviour in shops in the broader social context in their local area; and could gather information, eg through surveys or visits to shops, to complement the picture available from officially reported crime. Effort to increase the reporting of crime etc should proceed in parallel. Joint working between a force's crime prevention department and its community involvement department (which are often under the same overall command) may be useful in all these respects.

(c)   The strategy might involve giving priority to harder-hit shops and to some outreach work, involving visits or the distribution of leaflets, rather than waiting for shopkeepers to seek help and then operating purely on a demand-led, 'first-come-first-served' basis. To begin with shops selling alcohol, or shops in isolated positions, could be approached.

(d)   The advice given to shopkeepers both nationally and locally could be extended to include ways of avoiding assault and avoiding or containing disputes or harassment. It may be worth exploring the market for producing leaflets in Asian language versions.

(e)   Shopkeepers suffering a fairly high rate of trouble should be encouraged to keep a simple log of incidents containing information on the nature of the offence, timing, method etc. This could be initiated with the help of a CPO, kept over a month or two and then jointly considered as a basis for devising preventive measures targeted on the requirements of the individual shop.

(f)   It may be worth setting up local self-help groups of shopkeepers whose aim would be to identify particular local problems, develop and implement ways of preventing them, and offer mutual support — perhaps in the context of Business Watch organisations or chambers of commerce. The police and other agencies could participate on an advisory or supporting basis. There may be some benefit from running such a scheme as a national demonstration project.

These measures could help to increase shopkeepers' confidence in their ability both to cope with racial hostility and to prevent crime motivated from other sources. Because small shops are often focal points for their neighbourhoods, both socially and economically, the effects of better relationships and increased confidence could spread.

The results of this study suggest that some of the offensive behaviour suffered by Asian shopkeepers can be seen as having closer connections with materialistic crimes and disputes than might have been assumed. Some scope therefore exists for prevention by conventional means such as target hardening or changes in business practices. But racial harassment and racially-motivated materialistic crime also call for action by the wider community, including the police and other social agencies. The Association of Chief Police Officers in January 1986 emphasised the duty of the police to deal with the perpetrators of racial attacks and to gain the confidence of ethnic minority communities. Since January 1987 efforts by the Metropolitan Police have included the establishment of racial incident panels in parts of London, including Newham. The preventive role of the police can usefully extend beyond the crime prevention specialism to include a broadly-based commitment on the part of local officers to tackle racial attacks and harassment, and to be seen to be doing so by all sections of the community. Some racial harassment, of course, may only succumb to long-term social measures beyond the scope of police action.

For the Asian victims interviewed in this study, crime and racial hostility overlapped, both in what they experienced and in how they perceived these experiences. Many small shops are run by Asians. Because of these conjunctions, all who are concerned with crime prevention in such premises should be aware of the possible racial implications.

Appendix 1: Additional Tables

Table A1.1: Statistics describing the four areas.

This table has used statistics to derive some figures intended as social indicators of differences between the four areas of the survey. All were taken from the 1981 Census except for unemployment rates, which refer to April 1987, and crime rates, which refer to 1984. The sources were: *Census 1981: Ward Monitor for Greater London* (OPCS, 1983); *Annual Abstract of Greater London Statistics 1984-85* (GLC, 1986); and unpublished figures supplied by the London Research Centre.

The crime rates were available only for each borough as a whole. The other indicators were compiled for the actual survey areas by the method described below. The items were defined as follows:

Ethnic groups: % of households whose heads were born in:

(1) I, P, B: India, Pakistan, Bangladesh

(2) A, C: Nigeria, Gambia, Ghana, Sierra Leone, Zimbabwe, Botswana, Lesotho, Swaziland and any British Commonwealth Caribbean country

(3) UK, I   UK, Republic of Ireland, Isle of Man

These 3 groupings do not include all Asian, Afro-Caribbean, and white residents, because (a) they omit certain countries, (b) they refer only to heads of households, (c) they do not distinguish ethnicity among households whose heads were born in Britain. But they are sufficient to show relative differences between the 4 areas.

Housing and amenities: % of households:

(4) O.OC: owning the dwelling they occupy

(5) Car: having the use of a car or van

Social class: % of households whose head is:

(6) I, II: Professional and intermediate

(7) IV, V: Semi skilled and unskilled.

Unemployment: (8): % of economically active persons unemployed at April 1987.

For each item (1)−(8) the statistic was obtained for all wards where there were any of the shops identified for the survey. Then a composite indicator was derived by weighting the statistic for each ward by the number of sampled shops in it, and taking the mean. Thus, for example, the ''I, P, B'' figure for ''Muswell Hill'' is weighted towards the proportion of Asian residents in the centre of the area, but also contains a small element reflecting the different neighbourhoods on its outskirts from which a few of the sample were drawn.

26

Table A1.1 (a): Composite indicators for the 4 survey areas

	"Muswell Hill" %	"Brixton" %	"Brent" %	"Newham" %
Ethnic groups				
(1) I, P, B	2.1	1.5	7.5	8.1
(2) A, C	5.1	18.6	8.7	9.5
(3) UK, I	77.0	69.2	68.9	77.0
Housing and amenities				
(4) O.OC	47.3	23.3	59.8	36.3
(5) Car	54.5	37.3	56.4	42.7
Social class				
(6) I, II	31.0	14.5	21.5	12.4
(7) IV, V	10.3	21.5	12.2	20.9
(8) Unemployment	12.6	21.4	12.0	17.8

Table A1.1 (b): Crime rates for the 4 London Boroughs

	Haringey	Lambeth	Brent	Newham
Notifiable offences known to police per 1000 estimated mid-year home population, 1984	111	164.5	77.3	112.5

Table A1.2: Burglary (and attempts): prevalence and estimated incidence

Total no. of shopkeepers (100%)	240
No. who had been burgled:	
within the last month	7
1 to 3 months ago	9
3+ to 6 months ago	11
6+ to 9 months ago	8
9+ to 12 months ago	14
No. inf. as to when	3
Total prevalence within 1 year	1
As % of shopkeepers	22%

In this sample the data seem to accord reasonably well with the assumption that the number of burglaries per shopkeeper is distributed as a Poissonian random variable. Then the incidence, defined as the average number of burglaries per shopkeeper per year, can be estimated as follows: incidence=log e (1 −prevalence) where prevalence = proportion of shopkeepers burgled at least once during the year.

Estimated incidence in this case is 0.24; this means that the average Asian shopkeeper among those interviewed here would be burgled about once every 4 years.

Table A1.3 Assaults: prevalence and estimated incidence

Total no. of shopkeepers	**240**
No. assaulted:	
within the last month	4
1 to 3 months ago	9
3+ to 6 months ago	4
6+ to 9 months ago	3
9+ to 12 months ago	8
Total prevalence within 1 year	28
As % of shopkeepers	12%
Estimated incidence (calculated as for Table A1.2)	0.12

The estimate is that the average Asian shopkeeper would be assaulted about once in every 8 or 9 years.

Table A1.4: Estimated incidence of burglary and assault, by area

Total no. of shopkeepers	Muswell Hill 49	Brixton 64	Brent 64	Newham 63
Estimated incidence per shopkeeper within one year (using the same method as in Tables A1.2 and A1.3)				
burglary	0.31	0.21	0.35	0.14
assault	0.11	0.19	0.06	0.14

Table A1.5: Crime prevention measures taken by shopkeepers

Total no. of shopkeepers	240	
Those who said they took the following measures:	No.	%
Shop Layout		
positioning of shelves/gondolas	106	44
positioning of tills/counters	108	45
any other	6	3
Business practices		
employ extra staff mainly to prevent trouble —		
all the time	10	4
at specific times	15	6
restrict opening hours	29	12
watch certain individuals/customer types closely	69	29
limit or keep out certain individuals/customer types	13	5
follow practices likely to avoid/reduce disputes	31	13
take special care when cashing up	122	51
Technological methods		
video cameras	17	7
burglar alarms	126	53
attack alarms	41	17
mirrors	157	65
window/door grilles/shutters	160	67
toughened glass windows	34	14
security window locks	80	33
security door locks	117	49
letter box protection	40	17
dummy video cameras, burglar alarms etc	7	3
Other measures		
deterrent notices	8	3
dogs or other animals	40	17
personal defence:		
weapons available	10	4
any other	4	2
Don't know	11	5

Table A1.6: Insurance against crime

		No.	%
Total no. of shopkeepers		**240**	
Those who said they were insured against:		No.	%
everything/all the usual		22	9
theft/stealing		88	37
robbery		27	11
burglary/break-ins		44	18
assault/injury to staff/attack etc		102	43
window damage/damage/vandalism		63	26
fire/arson		48	20
money on way to bank/money stolen/till		29	12
stock/goods/contents		18	8
other answers		16	7
no type stated		10	4
All who were insured:	No.	193	
	%	80	
Don't know whether any insurance:	No.	27	
	%	11	
Not insured at all:	No.	20	
	%	8	

Appendix 2: Experiences of white and black shopkeepers

Among the original aims of this study had been an attempt to compare the crime and related incidents experienced by the three major ethnic groups of shopkeepers — Asian, white and black. The introduction (page 1) described the difficulties which led to the abandonment of these comparisons: principally the small numbers of non-Asian shopkeepers found in the study areas, and the fact that the method of obtaining interviewees meant that representative samples of the groups were not drawn — rather, the sets of interviewees were more closely akin to populations than to samples at all. Picking the shopkeepers' ethnic groups out as a cause of differences in crimes described is not possible, because the ethnic groups were to be found in different proportions in different areas, and differed also in the siting of the shops and to some extent the type of goods sold. What can be said is that in general, Asians were more likely to own their shops than the other groups, suggesting that they had a greater stake in the successes of the store, and the problems, including crime.

Black shopkeepers in Brixton

Although the 18 black shopkeepers interviewed in Brixton comprise a very small group, as said they do constitute something approaching the population of black shopkeepers in that area. It is therefore felt of interest to describe selected aspects of their reported experiences.

Only one out of the 18 worried a lot about crime in and around the shop, and five a fair amount; 11 worried not very much or had no worry at all. Seven of those who were worried to some degree mentioned specific crimes like stealing, assault, burglary or robbery. The numbers of black shopkeepers reporting ever having suffered from the crimes and other problems in question are presented in Table A2.1.

Shop theft was the most frequently-cited problem, mentioned by eight of the black shopkeepers; four mentioned credit card/cheque fraud and three each robbery and window-smashing. None of the 11 who had suffered any problem said it was serious for the long term running and future of the store, and none felt any had been racially motivated. One had experienced a single incident of racial harassment in the last twelve months — shouting and swearing. Five of the 11 victims always reported crimes suffered to the police and one quite often; one not very often, two never and one depending on the seriousness of the incident.

A range of preventive measures were employed, with 10 of the 18 having fitted grilles or shutters, 8 taking special care when cashing up and 6 installing security door locks. Eleven had received no advice on prevention; one from a police CPO. Nine would like advice from the police but seven would not, indicating the need for sensitivity in approaches by CPOs. Eleven of the 18 were insured and seven uninsured, of whom one felt the cost was too high, but four found difficulty finding a company willing to take them on.

Table A2.1: Black shopkeepers' experience of particular crimes and other incidents in Brixton

Total no. of shopkeepers	**18**
Those who said they had ever suffered:	
arson, fire raising	1
snatch from till	—
price switching	1
theft of goods, shoplifting	8
cheque/credit card fraud	4
threatening behaviour	2
assault	1
theft by shop staff	—
murder	—
robbery	3
window smashing	3
graffiti	1
other damage	—
disputes with customers over:	
charging/change	2
credit	2
returned goods	2
verbal abuse	2
abusive phone calls	—
abusive/offensive letters/literature	—
none of these	7

White shopkeepers in ethnic minority areas

While the 32 white shopkeepers interviewed constituted a diverse and scattered group, their position as a minority in their own right in each area studied gives them enough in common to justify brief presentation of their responses to the questionnaire. How far the findings can be generalised to white shopkeepers in other areas, with proportionally fewer of their fellow shopkeepers stemming from the ethnic minorities, is unknown — another survey would be needed to settle this.

Seven out of the 32 worried a lot about crime in and around the shop, and seven a fair amount; five worried a little and 13 worried not very much or had no worry at all. Of those 19 who were worried to some degree 12 mentioned shop theft and stealing, and 3 or 4 mentioned burglary, robbery or assault. The numbers of white shopkeepers reporting ever having suffered from the crimes and other problems in question are presented in Table A2.2.

Table A2.2: White shopkeepers' experience of particular crimes and other incidents

Total no. of shopkeepers	**32**
Those who said they had ever suffered:	
arson, fire raising	1
snatch from till	8
price switching	3
theft of goods, shoplifting	23
cheque/credit card fraud	8
threatening behaviour	12
assault	5
theft by shop staff	5
murder	—
robbery	7
window smashing	11
graffiti	4
other damage	1
disputes with customers over:	
charging/change	9
credit	6
returned goods	4
verbal abuse	12
abusive phone calls	3
abusive/offensive letters/literature	1
none of these	3

Shop theft was the most frequently-cited problem, mentioned by 23; about a dozen each mentioned threatening behaviour, window smashing and verbal abuse. One each felt that till snatch, shoptheft, robbery and verbal abuse were serious threats to the long term running and future of the store. Crimes and other problems in which racial motivation was felt to have played a part on at least a quarter of occasions included threatening behaviour, assault, window smashing, graffiti, verbal abuse and disputes over charging/change and returned goods. Of the 29 victims, only 12 said they always or quite often reported crimes to the police; nine said they never did.

A wide range of preventive measures had been adopted, with shop layout and technological methods used most frequently, as well as surveillance of particular individuals or types of customer. Twenty-one had received no advice on prevention; 8 had received it, from a CPO. Twice as many wanted police advice as did not. Only five out of 32 were not insured against any form of crime, of whom only one had been refused and one found the cost too high.

Appendix 3: Relating the present results to the Newham Crime Survey

As the main text described, Asian shopkeepers in Newham showed a level of worry higher than that of their fellows in the other three areas; they were more likely to attribute crime to racial motives, and to insure themselves against assault (though little else). Yet according to their interview answers they actually suffered the lowest rates for crimes generally, and for burglary and racial harassment in particular. Only 3% reported racial harassment. Ninety-four percent could give the interviewer no specific reasons, connected with the shop, for their worries about crime.

The London Borough of Newham, in evidence to the Home Affairs Committee on racial attacks in 1986, suggested that the situation was far more serious: that 23% of a sample of households had suffered racial harassment, and that in a pilot survey a third of black and Asian residents had been victims of racially motivated crime during a year. Ethnic minorities, it was said, had little confidence in the police to deal effectively with racial attacks, and the Borough Council was itself taking action in various ways and calling on other agencies to do the same.

In 1986 the Council commissioned the Harris Research Centre to survey Newham residents, asking about their experiences and perceptions of crime, racial harassment, and policing. 'Ethnically matched' interviewers were used with the majority of Asian and Afro-Caribbean respondents, and this may have been an advantage, though in the main sample which included some of these respondents the response rate was only 59%.

The findings (London Borough of Newham, 1987) raise some questions about the results of the present study. For crimes not perceived as racial harassment, Newham residents' risks of being victims were not greatly different from those found by the BCS for other inner city areas: for example, the proportion of householders suffering burglary in the past year was reported as 12%. Asians were somewhat more likely to be victims of apparently non-racial crime than whites (the proportions suffering any of the surveyed offences was 20% for whites, 23% for Afro-Caribbeans, and 25% for Asians). But in addition 28% of Asians (and 22% of Afro-Caribbeans) said that during the year they had suffered racial harassment: half these incidents comprised insulting behaviour, and the other half were threatened, attempted, or actual occurrences of damage, assault or theft. Seventy-six percent of Asian residents said they worried "a great deal" or "a fair amount" about being a victim of crime, 57% believed that racial attacks were common in Newham, and 79% said that "people being attacked or assaulted" should be among the top priorities for policing in the borough. Other findings indicated that many Asians had little confidence in the police to deal effectively with these problems.

Several explanations could be suggested for the apparent difference in amounts of crime and racial harassment reported by the Newham Council survey and the present study. First is that the Asian shopkeepers had in fact experienced more crime and harassment in their shops, but in Newham alone of the four areas studied did not have the confidence to tell the white interviewer about it.

Second, the present study was confined to the Stratford and Upton Park areas of Newham, whereas the Newham Survey covered the whole borough.

Third, it may be that the concern about racial incidents shown by the Council and other agencies in Newham, and the amount of local publicity, raised Asian shopkeepers' anxiety there to a higher level than existed in other areas. This would explain why they worried more, but not why they reported less crime.

Fourth, it is possible that the perpetrators of racial harassment, as distinct from non racially-motivated crime, more often attack victims in their homes than at their places of business. If it were so, the responses of Asian shopkeepers in the present study may well have been influenced by events that occurred elsewhere. They may have suffered relatively little in their shops, but anxiety about their family and friends affected their whole outlook. Whatever their actual experience, the level of worry expressed by many Asian shopkeepers, especially in Newham, is a very real problem that needs to be addressed.

Appendix 4: The Questionnaire

May I begin by asking you a few questions about the shop here.

Q1   *Looking at this list can you tell me which of these things does this shop sell or supply?*

        Alcohol
        Fresh meat
        Other food
        Newspapers and magazines
        Soft drinks and sweets
        Sub-Post Office services
        Tobacco
        Other

Q2a   *At what time is the shop normally opened for business during the week?*

        Before 6.15 am
        6.16 - 6.45 am
        6.46 - 7.15 am
        7.16 - 7.45 am
        7.46 - 8.15 am
        8.16 - 8.45 am
        8.46 - 9.15 am
        After 9.16 am
        Varies too much/Can't say

Q2b   *And at what time is the shop normally closed for business for the day?*

        Before 5.45 pm
        5.46 - 6.15 pm
        6.16 - 6.45 pm
        6.46 - 7.15 pm
        7.16 - 7.45 pm
        7.46 - 8.15 pm
        8.16 - 8.45 pm
        8.46 - 9.15 pm
        9.16 - 9.45 pm
        After 9.46 pm
        Varies too much/Can't say

Q3a   *Is this shop opened for business at all on a Sunday?*

        No
        Yes

If yes:

At what time is the shop normally opened for business on a Sunday?

> Before 6.15 am
> 6.16 - 6.45 am
> 6.46 - 7.15 am
> 7.16 - 7.45 am
> 7.46 - 8.15 am
> 8.16 - 8.45 am
> 8.46 - 9.15 am
> 9.16 - 9.45 am
> After 9.46 am
> Varies too much/Can't say

Q3b *And at what time is the shop normally closed for business on a Sunday?*

> Before 12.15 pm
> 12.16 - 1.15 pm
> 1.16 - 2.15 pm
> 2.16 - 3.15 pm
> 3.16 - 4.15 pm
> 4.16 - 5.15 pm
> 5.16 - 6.15 pm
> 6.16 - 7.15 pm
> 7.16 - 8.15 pm
> 8.16 - 9.15 pm
> After 9.16 pm
> Varies too much/Can't say

To all:

Q4a *At any one moment in time what is the typical number of people, including yourself, who are working here? Please include both full-time staff and anyone else, such as members of your family, who may help out at any stage during the week.*

Q4b *And across the week how many **different** people in total work in this shop?*

Q5 *Do you live at this address?*

> Yes
> No

Q6a *Are you the owner of this business?*

> Yes
> No

If no:

Q6b   *Can you tell me what is your relationship with the owner of this shop?*

        Family relative
        Employee/Shop Manager
        Other

To all:

Q7   *Is this a fully independent shop, a franchise operation, part of a marketing and buying chain, or a fully owned part of a chain?*

        Independent
        Franchise
        Marketing/Buying chain
        Fully owned chain
        Don't know

Q8   *Are your customers mostly white, mostly Asian, or mostly African and West Indian?*

        Mostly white
        Mostly Asian
        Mostly African/West Indian
        A mixture
        Don't know

Now I would like to talk to you about the subject of crime and the ways in which it may affect your running of this shop.

Q9   *Is the risk of crime in and around the shop something that you worry about at all?*

    If yes:

    Would you say it worries you a lot, a fair amount, a little, or really not very much at all?

        A lot
        A fair amount
        A little
        Not very much at all
        No worry
        Don't know

Q10   *What types of crime in and around the shop do you most worry about?*

    And what others?

Q11   When do you feel most at risk from crime?

       And at any other times?

Q12   Are there any particular sources of trouble for the shop in the local area that
       concern you?

       And what others?

       I should now like to talk about criminal or other problems that you might have
       experienced recently.

Q13   Looking at this list of incidents can you tell me which, if any, of these you or
       other members of the staff have **ever** suffered from in this shop?

            Arson, fire raising
            Snatch from the till
            Price switching
            Theft of goods/shop-lifting
            Cheque/credit card fraud
            Threatening behaviour
            Assault
            Theft by shop staff
            Murder
            Robbery
            Window smashing
            Graffiti
            Other damage
            Dispute with customer over:
                 Charging or Change
                 Credit
                 Returned goods
            Verbal abuse
            Abusive phone calls
            Abusive/offensive letters/literature
            None of these

       If any:

Q14   For each of the incidents you or other members of the staff have ever suffered
       from can you tell me about how often they happen? Do they happen:

            Almost every day
            About once a week
            About once in a month
            Just a few times a year

       or are they very rare events indeed happening less than once a year.

Q15　For each type of incident you or other members of the staff have suffered from can you now tell me about how many of them you feel have been racially motivated:

> None
> About a quarter
> About half
> About three quarters
> All of them?

Q16　Which, if any, of the incidents you and your staff have suffered from in this would you describe as 'serious problems' for the long term running and future of the store?

Q17　How often do you report the crimes you have suffered to the police?

> Always
> Quite often
> Not very often
> Never
> It depends

If never/not very often:

Q18a　What reasons do you have for never/not very often reporting crimes to the police?

Any others?

If it depends:

Q18b　What does it depend on?

Anything else?

To all:

I would now like to ask you some questions on crime prevention.

Q19　Looking at this list can you tell me which of these measures, if any, you take at present to prevent crimes by customers and other people not connected to the shop, (in other words everybody excluding employees and deliverymen)?

> *Shop Layout*
>
> > Positioning of shelves/gondolas
> > Positioning of tills/counters
> > Any other

Business Practices

Employ extra staff mainly to prevent trouble

— All the time
— At specific times
— when?

Restrict opening hours
Watch certain individuals/customer types closely

— which?

Limit or keep out certain individuals/customer types

— which?

Follow practices likely to avoid/reduce disputes
Take special care when cashing up

Technological methods

Video cameras
Burglar alarms
Attack alarms
Mirrors
Window/door grilles/shutters
Toughened glass windows
Security window locks
Security door locks
Letter box protection
Dummy video cameras, burglar alarms etc.

Other measures:

Deterrent Notices: eg Shoplifting is theft
Personal defence: weapons available

— what type

Dogs or other animals
Any other
Don't know

Q20   *Have you received advice on crime prevention from anyone?*

No
Yes

If yes: who have you received such advice from?

Police/Crime Prevention Officer
Insurance Company Consultant
Independent Consultant

Security company
Friends/fellow shopkeepers
Chain partners/franchisors
Other
Don't know/can't recall

Q21a *Were you satisfied with the advice you received?*

Yes
No
Don't know

Q21b *Why do you say that?*

Any other reasons?

If police/CPO not mentioned at Q20

Q22a *Is crime prevention advice from the police something that you would like to have?*

Yes
No
Don't know

If yes:

Q22b *Would you prefer the information from a visit by a police Crime Prevention Officer or by being sent leaflets about crime prevention?*

Police
Leaflets
Both
Don't know

If shopkeeper is Asian:

Q22c *Would you like such advice to be written in English or in an Asian language?*

English
Asian language
Don't mind which
Don't know

To all:

Q23 *Are there any things that have prevented or made it difficult for you to take or adopt any crime prevention measures?*

What are these?

Q24a Turning now to insurance cover, are you insured against any types of criminal activity?

      Yes
      No
      Don't know

If no:

Q24b Why do you not have any insurance cover against criminal activity?

      What other reasons?

If yes:

Q24c What types of criminal activity are you insured against?

      What else?

Q25a Have the requirements of your insurance cover influenced any of the crime prevention measures you take?

      Yes
      No
      Don't know

Q25b What are or were these?

      Any others?

Q25c And about how much did these measures cost to install?

      Under £25
            £26-£100
            £101-£500
            £501-£1000
            £1001 +
            Don't know

Q26a Are there any regular running costs for these measures?

      Yes
      No
      Don't know

Q26b And about how much are these running costs per year?

      Under £26
            £26-£50
            £51-£100

£101-£200
£201 +
Don't know

To all:

I should now like to talk in a little more detail about some different types of incident that you may have suffered from in this shop.

Q27a *I should like to begin by talking about burglary, but may I first say exactly what I mean by burglary. This is when someone **enters** the shop as a **trespasser** with intention, whether or not they achieve it, of committing theft, greivous bodily harm or criminal damage. This would almost certainly take place when the shop is closed.*

Have you suffered a burglary here in the shop (not residential premises) in the last 12 months?

Yes
No
Don't know

If No/Don't know:

Q27b *Have you suffered an **attempted** burglary here in the shop in the last 12 months?*

Yes
No
Don't know

If yes to burglary or attempt:

Q28 *How long ago did the incident occur? (If more than one refer to most recent for Q28 — 40).*

Within last month
1- 3 months ago
3 + - 6 months ago
6 + - 9 months ago
9 + - 12 months ago

Q29 *Please **briefly** describe the incident.*

Q30a *Did you report the crime to the Police?*

Yes
No
Don't know

44

If no:

Q30b   What reasons did you have for not reporting the crime?

        What other reasons?

Q31   Do you know anything about the person or people who carried out this
        burglary?

        Yes
        No/Don't know

If yes:

Q32   Do you know how many people took part in the burglary?

        One
        Two
        Three
        Four or more
        Don't know

Q33   Do you know the approximate age(s) of the burglar(s)?

        15 or under
        16-20
        21-25
        26-35
        36-45
        46+
        Don't know

Q34   Do you know what race the burglars were?

        White
        Asian
        West Indian/African
        Other
        Don't know

Q35   Do you know were the burglars male or female?

        Male
        Female
        Both
        Don't know

Q36a   *What do you think was the main motivation behind the incident?*

Q36b *Why do you think this was the main motivation?*

What other reasons?

If racial motivation not mentioned:

Q37a *Do you think there was any racial motivation in this incident?*

If yes:

Q37b *Why do you think this?*

What other reasons?

Q38 *Why do you think this shop was picked rather than others?*

Any other reasons?

Q39 *What measures, if any, are you now taking to prevent burglary from happening again?*

What others?

Q40a *Were you insured against burglary at all before this crime happened?*

    Yes
    No
    Don't know

If yes:

Q40b *Did you claim on your insurance cover for this crime?*

    Yes
    No
    Don't know

If yes:

Q40c *About how much of the value of your loss was covered by the insurance?*

    None/claim rejected
    About a quarter
    About half
    About three quarters
    Nearly all
    The full value
    Don't know

To all:

Q41   *Could we now consider assault. Have you or anyone else working here experienced an assault in connection with this shop in the last 12 months?*

    (excluding assaults linked to a burglary)

        Yes
        No
        Don't know

    If yes:

Q42   *How long ago did the incident occur? (If more than one refer to most recent for Q42 — 55)*

        Within last month
        1 - 3 months ago
        3 + - 6 months ago
        6 + - 9 months ago
        9 + - 12 months ago

Q43   *Please briefly describe the incident.*

Q44a   *What type of injury did you/the member of staff receive?*

    Any further injuries?

    If injured:

Q44b   *Do you think the attacker intended to injure you/the member of staff?*

        Yes
        No
        Don't know

Q45a   *Did you report the crime to the Police?*

        Yes
        No
        Don't know

    If no:

Q45b   *What reasons did you have for not reporting the crime?*

    What other reasons?

Q46   *Do you know anything about the people who carried out this assault?*

> Yes
> No
> Don't know

If yes:

Q47   *Do you know how many people took part in this assault?*

> One
> Two
> Three
> Four or more
> Don't know

Q48   *Do you know the approximate age(s) of the person/people who made this assault?*

> 15 or under
> 16-20
> 21-25
> 26-35
> 36-45
> 46+
> Don't know

Q49   *Do you know what race the attackers were?*

> White
> Asian
> West Indian/African
> Other
> Don't know

Q50   *Were the attackers male or female?*

> Male
> Female
> Both
> Don't know

Q51a   *What do you think was the main motivation behind the incident?*

Q51b   *Why do you think this was the main motivation?*

What other reasons?

If racial motivation not mentioned:

Q52a *Do you think there was any racial motivation in this incident?*

> Yes, definitely
> Yes, probably/maybe
> No
> Don't know

If yes:

Q52b *Why do you think this?*

Any other reasons?

Q53 *Why do you think this shop was picked rather than others?*

What other reasons?

Q54 *What measures, if any, are you taking to prevent assault from happening again?*

What others?

Q55a *Were you insured against assault at all before this crime happened?*

> Yes
> No
> Don't know

If yes:

Q55b *Did you claim on your insurance cover for this crime?*

> Yes
> No
> Don't know

If yes:

Q55c *About how much of the value of your loss was covered by the insurance?*

> None/claim rejected
> About a quarter
> About half
> About three quarters
> Nearly all
> The full value
> Don't know

To all:

Q56a   *Could we now consider racial harassment. This could be a series of incidents which you think may be linked and which you believe were carried out by people with racial motives.*

Have you or anyone else here experienced such a series of incidents of racial harassment in the shop in the last 12 months?

    Yes
    No
    Don't know

If no/don't know:

Q56b   *Have you or anyone else here experienced racial harassment in the form of a **single** incident in the last 12 months?*

    Yes
    No
    Don't know

If yes to series or single incident:

Q57   *Please briefly describe the (series of) incident(s) from the start. (If more than one series refer to most recent for Q57 — 67)*

Q58   *Why do you consider this (series of) incident(s) was racially motivated?*

What other reasons?

Q59a   *Did you report this to the police?*

    Yes
    No
    Don't know

If no:

Q59b   *What reasons did you have for not reporting this incident?*

What other reasons?

Q60   *Do you know anything about the person or people who carried out this incident?*

    Yes
    No
    Don't know

If yes:

Q61   *Do you know how many people took part in this racial harassment?*

        One
        Two
        Three
        Four or more
        Don't know

Q62   *Do you know the approximate age(s) of the person/people involved?*

        15 or under
        16-20
        21-25
        26-35
        36-45
        46+
        Don't know

Q63   *Do you know what race the offenders were?*

        White
        Asian
        West Indian/African
        Other
        Don't know

Q64   *Were the offenders male or female?*

        Male
        Female
        Both
        Don't know

Q65   *What measures, if any, are you now taking to prevent such things from happening again?*

What others?

Q66   *Were you insured against the effects of racial harassment at all before the incident happened?*

        Yes
        No
        Don't know

If yes:

Q67a *Did you claim on your insurance cover for this incident?*

      Yes
      No
      Don't know

If yes:

Q67b *About how much of the value of your loss was covered by the insurance?*

      None/claim rejected
      About a quarter
      About half
      About three quarters
      Nearly all
      The full value
      Don't know

To all:

*Finally, may I ask you, if it can be arranged, would you be interested in having a visit from a crime prevention officer during the next few weeks. He will survey your premises and recommend appropriate crime prevention measures. This service is free and without obligation. The police will **not** see the answers you have given me here. The researchers, though, would like to see the Crime Prevention Officer's report of his visit.*

Q68 *Would you like a visit from a Police Crime Prevention Officer?*

      Yes
      No
      Don't know

If yes:

Q69 *May the researchers see the Crime Prevention Officer's report on your premises?*

      Yes
      No
      Don't know

References

Bottoms, A.E., Mawby, R.I., and Walker, M.A. (1987). 'A Localised Crime Survey in Contrasting Areas of a City'. *British Journal of Criminology*, 27, pp. 125-154.

Burrows, J. (1988). *Retail crime: prevention through crime analysis.* Crime Prevention Unit Paper 11. London: Home Office.

Ekblom, P. (1986). *The prevention of shop theft: an approach through crime analysis.* Crime Prevention Unit Paper 5. London: Home Office.

Greater London Council Intelligence Unit (1986). *Annual Abstract of Greater London Statistics 1984-85.* London: GLC.

Home Office (1981). *Racial Attacks: report of a Home Office study.* London: Home Office.

Home Office (1984). *Crime Prevention. Circular 8/1984.* 30 January.

Home Office (1986). *Profit from Prevention: a guide to preventing theft in smaller shops and retail outlets.* London: HMSO.

Home Office (1986). *The Prevention of Violence Associated with Licensed Premises: report of the Working Group of the Standing Conference on Crime Prevention.* London: Home Office.

Hough, M. and Mayhew, P. (1985). *Taking Account of Crime: Key findings from the second British Crime Survey.* Home Office Research Study No. 85. London: HMSO.

House of Commons Home Affairs Committee (1986). *Third Report: Racial Attacks and Harassment.* London: HMSO.

Independent Grocer, 27 September 1985, pp. 11-13; 11 October 1985, p22.

London Borough of Newham (1987). *Crime in Newham: the Survey.* London: Policing and Community Safety Unit, Newham Borough Council.

Office of Population Censuses and Surveys (1982). *Census 1981: OPCS County Monitors for Outer and Inner London; County Report for Greater London.* London: HMSO.

Office of Population Censuses and Surveys (1984). *Census 1981: Key Statistics for Local Authorities.* London: HMSO.

Scarman, Lord (1981). *The Brixton Disorders 10-12 April 1981.* Report of an inquiry by the Rt. Hon. The Lord Scarman, OBE. Cmnd. 8427. London: HMSO.

Shapland, J. and Vagg, J. (1985). *Social Control and Policing in Rural and Urban Areas.* (Final report to the Home Office, unpublished).

Crime Prevention Unit Papers

1. **Reducing Burglary: a study of chemists' shops.**
   Gloria Laycock. 1985. v + 7 pp. (0 86353 154 8).

2. **Reducing Crime: developing the role of crime prevention panels.**
   Lorna J. F. Smith and Gloria Laycock. 1985. v + 14 pp. (0 86252 189 0).

3. **Property Marking: a deterrent to domestic burglary?**
   Gloria Laycock. 1985. v + 25 pp. (0 86252 193 9).

4. **Designing for Car Security: towards a crime free car.**
   Dean Southall and Paul Ekblom. 1985. v + 25 pp. (0 86252 222 6).

5. **The Prevention of Shop Theft: an approach through crime analysis.**
   Paul Ekblom. 1986. v + 19 pp. (0 86252 237 4).

6. **Prepayment Coin Meters: a target for burglary.**
   Nigel Hill. 1986. v + 15 pp. (0 86252 245 5).

7. **Crime in Hospitals: diagnosis and prevention.**
   Lorna J. F. Smith. 1987. v + 25 pp. (0 86252 267 6).

8. **Preventing Juvenile Crime: the Staffordshire Experience.**
   Kevin Heal and Gloria Laycock. 1987. v + 29 pp. (0 86252 297 8).

9. **Preventing Robberies at Sub-Post Offices: an evaluation of a security
   initiative.** Paul Ekblom. 1987. v + 34 pp. (0 86252 300 1).

10. **Getting the Best Out of Crime Analysis.**
    Paul Ekblom. 1988. v + 38 pp. (0 86252 307 8).

11. **Retail Crime: Prevention through Crime Analysis.**
    John Burrows. 1988. v + 30pp (0 86252 313 3).

12. **Neighbourhood Watch in England and Wales: a locational analysis.**
    Sohail Husain. 1988. v + 63pp (0 86252 314 1).

13. **The Kirkholt Burglary Prevention Project, Rochdale.** David Forrester, Mike
    Chatterton and Ken Pease with the assistance of Robin Brown. 1988. v + 34pp
    (086252 333 8).

14. **The Prevention of Robbery at Building Society Branches.** Claire Austin.
    1988. v + 18pp (086252 337 0).